The Transforming Power of Scripture

The Transforming Power of Scripture

by
John MacArthur, Jr.

WORD OF GRACE COMMUNICATIONS
P.O. Box 4000
Panorama City, CA 91412

In chapter 1 all Scripture quotations, unless noted otherwise, are from the *New Scofield Reference Bible*, King James Version. Copyright © 1967 by Oxford University Press, Inc. Reprinted by permission.

In chapters 2-4 all Scripture quotations, unless noted otherwise, are from the *New American Standard Bible*, © 1960, 1962, 1963, 1968, 1971, 1972, 1973, 1975, and 1977 by The Lockman Foundation, and are used by permission.

ISBN: 0-8024-5372-4

1 2 3 4 5 Printing/LC/Year 91 90 89

Printed in the United States of America

Contents

These Bible studies are taken from messages delivered by Pastor-Teacher John MacArthur, Jr., at Grace Community Church in Panorama City, California. These messages have been combined into a 4-tape album titled *The Transforming Power of Scripture*. You may purchase this series either in an attractive vinyl cassette album or as individual cassettes. To purchase these tapes, request the album *The Transforming Power of Scripture*, or ask for the tapes by their individual GC numbers. Please consult the current price list; then, send your order, making your check payable to:

WORD OF GRACE COMMUNICATIONS
P.O. Box 4000
Panorama City, CA 91412

Or call the following toll-free number:
1-800-55-GRACE

1
The Doctrine of Scripture

Outline

Introduction

Lesson
I. Claims of Scripture About Itself
    A. It Is Infallible
        1. Defined
        2. Documented
            a) Psalm 19:7-9
            b) Psalm 119:160
            c) Matthew 5:17-18
            d) John 10:35
            e) Romans 7:12
    B. It Is Inerrant
        1. Defined
        2. Distinguished from infallibility
    C. It Is Authoritative
        1. Defined
        2. Documented
            a) Isaiah 1:2
            b) Revelation 19:9; 21:5
    D. It Is Complete
        1. Deuteronomy 4:2
        2. Revelation 22:18-19
        3. Jude 3
    E. It Is Effective
II. Verification of Scripture's Claims
    A. Internal Evidence
        1. The testimony of the biblical writers
            a) Galatians 1:11, 15
            b) 2 Peter 3:2

Introduction

A proper understanding of any area of theology depends upon the truthfulness of what God has revealed about Himself. If you deny the truthfulness of His Word, all that remains is human opinion. That's a hopeless resource for anyone seeking to know God.

Lesson

I. CLAIMS OF SCRIPTURE ABOUT ITSELF

The doctrine of Scripture is built upon the claims that the Bible makes for itself.

A. It Is Infallible

1. Defined

   The term *infallible* refers to the totality of Scripture; it makes no mistakes—it is without error in the truth it conveys.

2. Documented

   Although the actual word isn't found in Scripture, the concept of infallibility is applied to Scripture in many passages.

   a) Psalm 19:7-9

   King David said, "The law of the Lord is perfect. . . . the commandment of the Lord is pure. . . . the judgments of the Lord are true; they are righteous altogether" (NASB*).

   b) Psalm 119:160

   The psalmist said, "The sum of Thy word is truth, and every one of Thy righteous ordinances is everlasting" (NASB). All God's Word is true.

   c) Matthew 5:17-18

   Jesus said He didn't come to abolish the law or the prophets (labels describing the Old Testament) but to fulfill them. Indeed He promised that all would be fulfilled.

* *New American Standard Bible.*

d) John 10:35

Jesus also said that Scripture cannot be broken—its authority is binding.

e) Romans 7:12

The apostle Paul said, "The Law is holy, and the commandment is holy, and righteous and good" (NASB). That is a general statement confirming the infallibility of Scripture.

B. It Is Inerrant

1. Defined

Inerrant means "without error." Proverbs 30:5 says, "Every word of God is pure [flawless]."

2. Distinguished from infallibility

Infallibility refers to the totality of Scripture; inerrancy refers to its parts. The Bible is infallible in the truth it conveys because its words are without error. It can be trusted in its totality because each individual part is true.

God's Word is true because God is truthful. Scripture says that God cannot lie (Titus 1:2; Heb. 6:18). The prophet Jeremiah said, "The Lord is the true God [lit., "God of truth"]" (Jer. 10:10). The apostle John said, "God is true" (John 3:33). Jesus defined eternal life as knowing the only true God (John 17:3). In fact Jesus came so that people might "know him that is true . . . the true God, and eternal life" (1 John 5:20).

C. It Is Authoritative

1. Defined

The Bible has the authority of God Himself. When it speaks we are to listen and respond accordingly.

2. Documented

   a) Isaiah 1:2

      The prophet Isaiah said, "Hear, O heavens, and give ear, O earth; for the Lord hath spoken."

   b) Revelation 19:9; 21:5

      An angel said to John, "These are the true sayings of God. . . . These words are true and faithful."

Scripture is infallible and inerrant; therefore, it is authoritative.

D. It Is Complete

1. Deuteronomy 4:2

   Moses said, "Ye shall not add unto the word which I command you, neither shall you diminish anything from it." God forbids any altering of His Word.

2. Revelation 22:18-19

   John said, "I testify unto every man that heareth the words of the prophecy of this book [the book of Revelation], If any man shall add unto these things, God shall add unto him the plagues that are written in this book; and if any man shall take away from the words of the book of this prophecy, God shall take away his part from the tree of life, and out of the holy city, and from the things which are written in this book."

3. Jude 3

   "Earnestly contend for the faith which was once delivered unto the saints."

Scripture is complete. It is not to be increased or diminished.

E. It Is Effective

Isaiah said, "As the rain and the snow come down from heaven, and do not return there without watering the earth, and making it bear and sprout, and furnishing seed to the sower and bread to the eater; so shall My word be which goes forth from My mouth; it shall not return to Me empty, without accomplishing what I desire, and without succeeding in the matter for which I sent it" (Isa. 55:10-11, NASB). God's Word accomplishes its intended purposes.

The Bible claims to be infallible, inerrant, authoritative, complete, and effective. Those are amazing claims, but how do we know they're true?

II. VERIFICATION OF SCRIPTURE'S CLAIMS

The claims of Scripture are verified by both internal and external evidence.

A. Internal Evidence

1. The testimony of the biblical writers

For the most part the writers were common, everyday people, yet they claimed to be inspired by God. They spoke for Him without apology or self-consciousness.

a) Galatians 1:11, 15

Paul said, "I make known to you, brethren, that the gospel which was preached by me is not after man. For I neither received it of man, neither was I taught it, but by the revelation of Jesus Christ. . . . When it pleased God, who separated me from my mother's womb, and called me by his grace, to reveal his Son in me, that I might preach him among the Gentiles, immediately I conferred not with flesh and blood." Paul received his message directly from the Lord.

b) 2 Peter 3:2

Peter said, "Be mindful of the words which were spoken before by the holy prophets, and of the commandment of us, the apostles." Peter affirmed the authority of the Old Testament prophets, and equated the apostles' teachings with their teachings.

(See chapter 2 of this Bible study, pages 26-39, for a more detailed discussion of inspiration.)

2. The testimony of Jesus

As we have already seen, Jesus said that Scripture cannot be broken (John 10:35) and that every word will be fulfilled (Matt. 5:17-18). That wasn't all He said on the subject.

a) Matthew 26:24, 53-54

Speaking of His crucifixion, Jesus said, "The Son of man goeth as it is written of him" (v. 24). In the Garden of Gethsemane, He rebuked Peter's attempt to protect Him with a sword: "Thinkest thou that I cannot now pray to my Father, and he shall presently give me more than twelve legions of angels? But how, then, shall the scriptures be fulfilled, that thus it must be?" (vv. 53-54). Jesus knew Scripture had to be fulfilled and was unwilling to jeopardize its integrity even though that meant he would experience great personal sacrifice.

b) Mark 12:24

Jesus rebuked the Sadducees for their ignorance of Scripture: "Do ye not therefore err, because ye know not the scriptures, neither the power of God?" He acknowledged the importance and authority of Scripture and even quoted Exodus in his answer to the Sadducees' question.

c) Luke 16:17

Jesus said, "It is easier for heaven and earth to pass, than one tittle of the law to fail."

Would Jesus Deceive Us?

Jesus affirmed the truth of Scripture, so if it has errors, He didn't know about them or He covered them up. In either case He could not be God because God knows everything and He would never deceive us. On the other hand, the inerrancy of Scripture corresponds with the character of Jesus and the claims of His Word. Which view do you affirm?

3. The testimony of the Holy Spirit

Paul said, "Eye hath not seen, nor ear heard, neither have entered into the heart of a man, the things which God hath prepared for them that love him. But God hath revealed them unto us by his Spirit. . . . Now we have received, not the spirit of the world, but the Spirit who is of God; that we might know the things that are freely given to us of God. Which things also we speak, not in the words which man's wisdom teacheth, but which the Holy Spirit teacheth, comparing spiritual things with spiritual" (1 Cor. 2:9-10, 12-13). The Spirit of God gives testimony to the Word.

People cannot affirm the truth of Scripture apart from the Spirit's ministry in their hearts. To illustrate that point, I wrote the following paragraphs in the preface to my book *Why I Trust the Bible* (Wheaton, Ill.: Victor, 1983):

"It is not easy to convince unbelievers that the Bible is the Word of God on the basis of its unity, its scientific and historical accuracy, its miracles, and its archaeological evidence. In a special series spread over a three-week period, I presented such data at a private college in California. I thought the proof was overwhelming, yet to my knowledge not one person became a believer.

"Unbelievers cannot accept legitimate proof because they are blind to it. 'The natural man receiveth not the things of the Spirit of God; for they are foolishness unto him: neither can he know them, because they are spiritually discerned' (1 Cor. 2:14). Only as the Holy Spirit does His regenerating work—as He opens the mind, tears off the scales of blindness, gives life, and plants the understanding of God's revelation—only then do people believe the Bible is the Word of God and trust it. I know the Bible is true because the Spirit of God has convinced me of it.

"In light of this, I suggest a change in our approach. We have been saying, 'Prophecy has been fulfilled. The Bible is scientifically accurate. Miracles were performed. The biblical message of salvation through faith in Jesus Christ results in a revolutionary change in the lives of persons who believe. Because of all of these proofs,' we reason, 'the Bible is the Word of God.' Instead, I propose that we declare, 'The Bible is the Word of God; therefore, prophecy has been fulfilled, miracles have taken place, scientific statements are correct, and lives here have been transformed.' "

B. External Evidence

  1. The testimony of changed lives

   A believer's transformed life gives credibility to the gospel and can have a profound impact on an unbeliever. Many people have become Christians after seeing the power of God's Word at work in the life of a relative or friend.

   Now that's an acceptable argument in one sense, but it's weak in another. If you base all your beliefs upon experience, you will run into trouble. Followers of Mohammed, Buddha, and Hare Krishna can point to various experiences as the basis for their beliefs, but that doesn't necessarily mean that their beliefs are correct. Experience can help validate the power and authority of the Bible, but we do need more evidence.

  2. The testimony of science

   When the Bible speaks about a scientific subject it is always accurate.

a) Hydrology

Hydrology is the study of water's properties, distribution, and circulation on the earth and in the atmosphere. The Bible gives a detailed description of the hydrological cycle.

(1) Job 36:27-28

Elihu said, "[God] maketh small the drops of water; they pour down rain according to their vapor, which the clouds do drop and distill upon man abundantly."

(2) Psalm 135:7

David said, "[God] causeth the vapors to ascend from the ends of the earth," which is a description of evaporation.

(3) Job 26:8

Job said, "He bindeth up the waters in his thick clouds; and the cloud is not torn under them." Water comes down in the form of rain, ascends in the form of vapor, and is held in the clouds until it again descends to the earth.

(4) Job 28:10-11

Job said, "[God] cutteth out rivers among the rocks; and his eye seeth every precious thing. He bindeth the floods from overflowing." God established boundaries for the rivers and oceans.

(5) Psalm 33:7

David said, "[God] gathereth the waters of the sea together as an heap; he layeth up the depth in storehouses." God keeps the oceans in place.

b) Meteorology

Meteorology is the science of the atmosphere and atmospheric phenomena. Until the time of Galileo, it was not known that air has weight; yet thousands of years before Galileo, Job had said, "[God] looketh to the ends of the earth, and seeth under the whole heaven, to make the weight for the winds" (Job 28:24-25).

c) Astronomy

(1) The number of stars

In the seventeenth century, men like Kepler and Galileo gave birth to modern astronomy. Prior to that, the universe was generally thought to contain only about one thousand stars, which was the number that had been counted. Scientists now estimate that there are about 10^{25} stars (10 million billion billion) in the known universe (Henry M. Morris, *The Biblical Basis for Modern Science* [Grand Rapids: Baker, 1984], p. 156).

Jeremiah 31:37 says, "If heaven above can be measured, and the foundations of the earth searched out beneath, I will also cast off all the seed of Israel for all they have done, saith the Lord." God can no more turn His back on His covenant with Israel than a man can count all the stars or explore the center of the earth. Scientists make their best guesses about the number of stars but realize that they are innumerable (Gen. 15:5).

(2) The orbit of the sun

Scientists used to teach that the earth rotated around a stationary sun. But Scripture teaches that the sun's rotation is "from the end of the heaven, and [its] circuit unto the ends of it" (Ps. 19:6). Science has now caught up with Scripture, affirming that the earth orbits the sun, and the sun and earth together orbit within the universe (Robert Jastrow and Malcolm H. Thompson, *Astronomy: Fundamentals and Frontiers* [N.Y.: John Wiley & Sons, 1977], p. 6).

d) Geology

Geology is the study of the earth's history and composition.

(1) Isostasy

Isostasy is the study of the balance of the earth. For example, it's been discovered that the depths of the oceans must balance the heights of the mountains in order for the earth to rotate properly. Interestingly, the Bible says that God has "measured the waters in the hollow of his hand, and measured out heaven with the span . . . and weighed the mountains in scales, and the hills in a balance" (Isa. 40:12). Again we see a scientific truth conveyed in Scripture long before it was acknowledged as such.

(2) Geodesy

Geodesy is the branch of applied mathematics that deals with such things as the shape and size of the earth and the variations of terrestrial gravity. It used to be believed that the earth was flat, but the Bible has always affirmed its spherical shape.

(*a*) Isaiah 40:22

Isaiah said, "It is he who sitteth upon the circle of the earth."

(*b*) Job 38:14

The Lord said, "It [the earth] is turned like clay to the seal." Signatures used to be affixed to documents by means of a signature cylinder. Soft clay was placed onto the document;

then the cylinder was rolled over the clay leaving an impression of the writer's signature or seal. The cylinder had sticks attached to each end that served as handles. The Lord used that analogy as a picture of the earth turning on its axis.

(c) Job 26:7

The Bible teaches that the earth is suspended in space: "[God] . . . hangeth the earth upon nothing."

(See chapter 2 of this Bible study, pages 34-35, for a more detailed discussion of the testimony of science. For additional study about the Bible and science see Henry M. Morris, *The Biblical Basis for Modern Science* [Grand Rapids: Baker, 1984].)

3. The testimony of prophecy

I believe that fulfilled prophecy is the greatest evidence for the inspiration of Scripture, and the Bible is replete with such prophecies. The prophet Ezekiel prophesied that the city of Tyre would be utterly destroyed and never rebuilt (Ezek. 26-27). That's exactly what happened (see chapter 2, pp. 35-38 for additional details). He also prophesied that Sidon would be destroyed, then rebuilt (Ezek. 28:20-24). Sidon was located only twenty miles from Tyre, and Sidon was rebuilt and remains a seaport in Lebanon to this day. However, Tyre was never rebuilt. Ezekiel's prophecy has been fulfilled.

Ezekiel also gave specific prophecies against Egypt that came to pass (Ezek. 30:13-16), and the prophet Nahum said that the great city of Nineveh would be destroyed by a flood (Nahum 1:8). Students conducting archaeological studies at the sight of ancient Nineveh learned that the city was destroyed in the month of Ab, which is the rainy month. They found a stratum of pebbles and sand around the site, which verifies its destruction by flood (cf. Walter Maier, *The Book of Nahum: A Commentary* [St. Louis: Concordia, 1959], pp. 118-19).

There are many other prophecies that have been fulfilled with amazing accuracy, including more than three hundred prophecies about Jesus Christ. Fulfilled prophecy is a powerful witness to the truth of God's Word. (For further information and evidence, see Josh McDowell's *Evidence That Demands a Verdict* [San Bernardino, Calif.: Here's Life, 1979].)

Conclusion

God's Word is the infallible, inerrant, authoritative, complete, and effective source of divine truth. It gives wisdom, knowledge, and direction to those who believe and obey it. Sad to say, however, there are many people within the church whose commitment to biblical truth is so shallow that they have a minimal impact on an unbelieving world.

Theologian J. I. Packer wrote, "Certainty about the great issues of Christian faith and conduct is lacking all along the line. The outside observer sees us as staggering on from gimmick to gimmick and stunt to stunt like so many drunks in a fog, not knowing at all where we are or which way we should be going. Preaching is hazy; heads are muddled; hearts fret; doubts drain our strength; uncertainty paralyses action. We know the Victorian shibboleth that to travel hopefully is better than to arrive; and it leaves us cold. Ecclesiastics of certain type tell us that the wish to be certain is mere weakness of the flesh, a sign of spiritual immaturity, but we do not find ourselves able to believe them. We know in our bones that we were made for certainty, and cannot be happy without it. Yet, unlike the first Christians who in three centuries won the Roman world, and those later Christians who pioneered the Reformation, and the Puritan awakening, and the Evangelical revival, and the great missionary movement of the last century, we lack certainty. Why is this? We blame the external pressures of modern secularism but this is like Eve blaming the serpent. The real trouble is not in our circumstances, but in ourselves" (*God Has Spoken: Revelation and the Bible* [London: Hodder and Stoughton, 1965], pp. 11-12).

He's right! And the reason such a large segment of the church lacks certainty is that it doesn't believe that the Bible is really God's Word. There are also those who affirm the truth of Scripture, but don't act on it—they are practical atheists. How about you? I pray that you will have an unshakable confidence in God's Word and that others will see its transforming power at work in your life.

Focusing on the Facts

1. What does a proper understanding of theology depend upon (see p. 8)?
2. Define the word *infallible* (see p. 9).
3. How does the psalmist describe God's Word in Psalm 119:160 (see p. 9)?
4. What is the difference between infallibility and inerrancy (see p. 10)?
5. What is the appropriate response when God speaks (Isa. 1:2; see p. 11)?
6. What warning is given in Revelation 22:18-19 (see p. 11)?
7. From whom did Paul receive his gospel (Gal. 1:11, 15; see p. 12)?
8. People cannot affirm the truth of Scripture apart from the_____ _____ in their hearts (see p. 14).
9. What is the major weakness in using personal experience to verify the truth of Scripture (see p. 15)?
10. Define hydrology (see p. 16).
11. Define meteorology (see p. 17).
12. Define isostasy (see p. 18).
13. Explain the analogy used in Job 38:14 (see pp. 18-19).
14. What is the greatest evidence for the inspiration of Scripture (see p. 19)?
15. How was the city of Nineveh destroyed (Nahum 1:8; see p. 19)?

Pondering the Principles

1. Fulfilled prophecy is compelling evidence of the inspiration of Scripture. It is also a wonderful affirmation that God always keeps His promises. Read Matthew 6:25-33. What promises did Jesus make? How do those promises apply to your life? What condition did Jesus place on their fulfillment (v. 33)? Be sure to thank Him for His faithfulness in keeping His promises, and pray that He will keep you focused on the right priorities.

2. First Peter 3:15 says, "Always be prepared to give an answer to everyone who asks you to give the reason for the hope that you have" (NIV*). Apologetics is the field of study that equips us to defend the Christian hope and faith against secular criticism. Become proficient in that field by examining the books recommended in this chapter (see pages 19-20) and other books on the subject in your church library and local Christian bookstore. But once you have done so, remember that to obey 1 Peter 3:15 you must "do this with gentleness and respect, keeping a clear conscience, so that those who speak maliciously against your good behavior in Christ may be ashamed of their slander" (NIV).

* *New International Version.*

2
Our God-Breathed Bible

Outline

Introduction

Lesson
  I. Revelation
   A. Its Definition
   B. Its Means
     1. The Old Testament
     2. The New Testament
 II. Inspiration
   A. Its Origin
   B. Its Process
   C. Its Extent
   D. Its Distortions
     1. That Scripture is the product of human genius
       a) The view
       b) The response
     2. That Scripture is the product of dictation
       a) The view
       b) The response
     3. That Scripture is only partially inspired
       a) That only the thoughts are inspired
         (1) The view
         (2) The response
           (*a*) Old Testament examples
           (*b*) New Testament examples
       b) That only sacred topics are inspired
         (1) The view
         (2) The response
           (*a*) Figures of speech
           (*b*) Cultural differences

E. Its Evidence
  1. Science
     a) The matrix of existence
     b) The first law of thermodynamics
     c) The second law of thermodynamics
  2. Fulfilled prophecy
     a) The destruction of Tyre
     b) The judgment against Sidon
     c) Other prophecies
F. Its Benefit

Conclusion

Introduction

I hope you have a deep appreciation for the Bible. It is God's self-revelation to man—every word is from His mouth. Paul said, "All Scripture is inspired by God and profitable for teaching, for reproof, for correction, for training in righteousness; that the man of God may be adequate, equipped for every good work" (2 Tim. 3:16-17). Such a priceless treasure deserves our diligent study and disciplined obedience. That's why I teach the Bible systematically, paying attention to every detail.

Lesson

Revelation and inspiration are the processes by which God communicated His Word to mankind.

I. REVELATION

Hebrews 1:1-2 says, "God, after He spoke long ago to the fathers in the prophets in many portions and in many ways, in these last days has spoken to us in His Son."

A. Its Definition

Revelation is the act of making something known that was previously unknown. In the biblical sense it is divine disclosure. God has made Himself known through the Scriptures.

B. Its Means

Generally speaking, God revealed Himself by two means: Old Testament revelation ("long ago," v. 1) and New Testament revelation ("in His Son," v. 2).

1. The Old Testament

God spoke to the Jewish fathers through the Old Testament prophets. The Greek word translated "portions" (*polumerōs*) refers in this passage to the books of the Old Testament, whether historical, prophetic, or poetic. He also spoke in many ways: visions, prophecies, parables, types, symbols, ceremonies, theophanies, and by voice.

The Old Testament is not simply a collection of man's wisdom, the best of religious thinking, or the musings of godly people. It is God's Word—He is its author and theme. We see His identity, attributes, perspectives, commands, and blessings revealed through the people, places, and events it records. Sometimes His attributes are clearly described, as in the psalms. At other times He isn't even mentioned, yet He is the dominant presence throughout the book, as in Esther.

2. The New Testament

In the New Testament God spoke through His Son: the gospels record His life and teachings, Acts records the extension of His message through the apostles and the early church, the epistles teach the meaning and application of His life and ministry, and Revelation records His glorious return—the consummation of God's communication to this world.

Jesus promised His disciples that the Holy Spirit would teach them all things, remind them of His teachings, guide them into all truth, and disclose to them what was to come (John 14:26; 16:13). That was His promise of divine inspiration, and it extended to all New Testament writers.

Scripture is God's self-revelation; the means by which He guaranteed an accurate record of that revelation is inspiration. The Old Testament is the revelation of His holy character, divine attributes, and righteous law. The New Testament is God revealed in the person, nature, and work of His Son.

II. INSPIRATION

A. Its Origin

Second Peter 1:20 says, "Know this first of all, that no prophecy of Scripture is a matter of one's own interpretation." The Greek word translated "prophecy" here refers to a message rather than a prediction of the future. The word translated "interpretation" (Gk., *epilusis*) could mean "to release" (no message from Scripture is of one's own origin), or "to inspire" (no message of Scripture is a matter of one's own inspiration). Peter's usage of the genitive case suggests that he is referring to the origin rather than to the interpretation of Scripture. The idea is that nothing in Scripture came from a human source—it was all inspired by God.

B. Its Process

Second Peter 1:21 declares that "no prophecy was ever made by an act of human will, but men moved by the Holy Spirit spoke from God."

Scripture was not the product of any man's will. The word translated "made" and "moved" (Gk., *pherō*) means "to bear," "carry along," "convey," or "bring forth." It was used to describe a ship borne along in the water by the breeze in its sails. The Holy Spirit moved upon select individuals to enable them to speak and write the Word of God. He used their personalities, backgrounds, experiences, insights, vocabularies, and perceptions, but every word produced in the final product was the Word of God. That's the miracle of inspiration.

26

The process of inspiration is illustrated in God's call to Jeremiah. Jeremiah said, "The word of the Lord came to me saying, 'Before I formed you in the womb I knew you, and before you were born I consecrated you; I have appointed you a prophet to the nations.' Then I said, 'Alas, Lord God! Behold, I do not know how to speak, because I am a youth' " (Jer. 1:4-6).

God's response was immediate: "Then the Lord stretched out His hand and touched my mouth, and the Lord said to me, 'Behold, I have put My words in your mouth' " (v. 9). What a tremendous statement! That was God's promise to the writers of Scripture.

C. Its Extent

Inspiration includes the entire Bible. Paul said, "*All Scripture* is inspired by God" (2 Tim. 3:16, emphasis added). The Greek word translated "inspired" (*theopneustos*) means "God breathed." All Scripture is from the mouth of God, described as the "oracles of God" in Romans 3:2.

Inspiration and the Canon of Scripture

Some critics have wrongly suggested that the early church invented the canon of Scripture, or arbitrarily selected the books that are in our Bible. But the church didn't invent the canon any more than Newton invented the law of gravity. It simply acknowledged unique books with unique integrity and characteristics.

Although the canon of Scripture as we know it was not officially recognized until the Councils of Hippo (A.D. 393) and Carthage (A.D. 397), the inspired books were recognized, read, studied, and loved by Christians at the time of their writing. It was clear to the early church what was and was not the Word of God. Many erroneous books were excluded from the canon because they failed to measure up to the standards of an inspired book. (For information on those precise standards, see Norman L. Geisler and William E. Nix, *A General Introduction to the Bible* [Chicago: Moody, 1986], pp. 203-317.)

What Scripture Says, God Says

The biblical authors were so certain they were writing the actual Word of God that they often used the terms "God" and "Scripture" interchangeably.

1. Paul said, "The *Scripture*, foreseeing that God would justify the Gentiles by faith, preached the gospel beforehand to Abraham, saying, 'All the nations shall be blessed in you' " (Gal. 3:8, emphasis added). However, in Genesis 12:3 *God* is speaking to Abraham.

2. Paul said, "We preach to you the good news of the promise made to the fathers, that God has fulfilled this promise to our children in that He raised up Jesus, as it is also written in the second Psalm, 'Thou art My Son; today I have begotten Thee.' And as for the fact that He raised Him up from the dead, no more to return to decay, *He has spoken* in this way: 'I will give you the holy and sure blessings of David.' Therefore *He also says in another Psalm*, 'Thou wilt not allow Thy Holy One to undergo decay' " (Acts 13:32-35, emphasis added). Paul affirmed that God spoke through the psalms.

3. Romans 9:17 says, "The *Scripture says* to Pharaoh, 'For this very purpose I raised you up' " (emphasis added). However, in Exodus 9:16 *God* is speaking.

The biblical writers understood that when Scripture speaks, God speaks.

D. Its Distortions

There are many errant views of inspiration.

1. That Scripture is the product of human genius

   a) The view

   Some believe the Bible was written by men possessing a high level of human ability and religious genius similar to the great geniuses of music, literature, philosophy, and science.

b) The response

However, Scripture itself confirms that the biblical authors were not in themselves inspired. The Spirit of God used them at a specific time for a specific purpose. Only when God told them what He wanted spoken or written could they produce inspired writing (2 Pet. 1:20-21).

The Confidence and Authority of the Biblical Authors

The biblical writers knew that they wrote God's Word, and they did so with confidence and authority. They never apologized or tried to justify or defend themselves. Even though most of them did not have an extensive education and were in no earthly position to be respected as literary geniuses, they wrote with profound, supernatural wisdom and recorded accurate prophecies of future events. They also wrote about the character and purposes of God —calling their readers to submit to His authority which they revealed.

The New Testament writers affirmed the inspiration and authority of the Old Testament through numerous quotations and allusions. Paul described the law of God (the Old Testament Scriptures) as holy, righteous, and good (Rom. 7:12). The writers also cited or alluded to one another as authoritative agents of God's revelation (e.g., 2 Pet. 3:15-17). They knew they were writing the Word of God.

2. That Scripture is the product of dictation

a) The view

Some believe God dictated His revelation to the biblical authors, and they wrote it down word for word, much like stenographers.

b) The response

Although portions of the Bible were dictated (cf. Ex. 17:14; 34:27), the writers of Scripture weren't simply listening to a voice and mechanically writing every word. It is obvious that as God breathed His message into them He worked through their hearts, souls, minds, emotions, and experiences to produce the Word of God in the recognizable language of men.

3. That Scripture is only partially inspired

   a) That only the thoughts are inspired

      (1) The view

         Some believe that the biblical authors were inspired with great religious thoughts, which they wrote in their own words. Therefore, they assume that Bible study should focus on the concepts of Scripture rather than on the precise words.

      (2) The response

         Those holding this view are faced with a difficult question: How does one communicate thoughts without words? Such an idea is foreign to Scripture or to any other literature.

         (*a*) Old Testament examples

            The thoughts and concepts communicated by the Old Testament prophets were inextricably linked to the very words of God. When Moses sought to excuse himself from speaking God's words, the Lord said, "I will be with thy mouth, and teach thee what thou shalt say" (Ex. 4:12, KJV*). Jeremiah said, "The word of the Lord came to me" (Jer. 1:4). The Lord said to Ezekiel, "Son of man, take into your heart all My words which I shall speak to you, and listen closely. And go to the exiles, to the sons of your people, and speak to them" (Ezek. 3:10-11). Amos said, "I am not a prophet, nor am I the son of a prophet; for I am a herdsman

* King James Version.

and a grower of sycamore figs. But the Lord took me from following the flock and the Lord said to me, 'Go prophesy to My people Israel' " (Amos 7:14-15).

(b) New Testament examples

It was no different in the New Testament. Ananias said to Paul, "The God of our fathers has appointed you to know His will, and to see the Righteous One, and to hear an utterance from His mouth. For you will be a witness for Him" (Acts 22:14-15). John said, "I was in the Spirit on the Lord's day, and I heard behind me a loud voice . . . saying . . . 'Write therefore the things which you have seen, and the things which are, and the things which shall take place after these things' " (Rev. 1:10, 19).

Even Jesus, the Word made flesh, received His message from the Father (John 8:28). Isaiah said of Jesus, "[Jehovah] has made [His] mouth like a sharp sword" (Isa. 49:2) and "the Lord God has given [Him] the tongue of disciples" (Isa. 50:4). The Father taught the Son what to say.

The concept of thoughts without words is foolish. You might as well talk about a tune without notes, sun without light, a sum without figures, geology without rocks, or anthropology without men.

The Bible disproves the theory of inspired thoughts without inspired words. In fact, there were times when prophets wrote inspired words they did not fully understand. Peter said, "As to this salvation, the prophets who prophesied of the grace that would come to you made careful search and inquiry, seeking to know what person or time the Spirit of Christ within them was indicating as He predicted the sufferings of Christ and the glories to follow" (1 Pet. 1:10-11). In such cases the words of Scripture took precedence over the thoughts. How then can a theory of inspired thoughts without inspired words be rational?

The biblical position is clear: the very words of Scripture are inspired. That's why Jesus said, "Heaven and earth will pass away, but My words shall not pass away" (Matt. 24:35).

b) That only sacred topics are inspired

(1) The view

Some believe that the Bible is inspired when it speaks of sacred things but not when it speaks of secular things, such as science, history, and geography. They claim that historical, geographical, mathematical, and scientific facts in Scripture may be erroneous but say that need not concern Bible students, because inspiration applies to sacred issues, not secular.

(2) The response

Such a view makes a false distinction between sacred truth and secular truth. The Bible makes no such distinction and claims authority and inspiration in everything it says.

A misunderstanding of figures of speech and cultural differences are two errors that give rise to this view.

(a) Figures of speech

Many figures of speech are used in the Bible. For example, Joshua 10:13 says, "The sun stopped in the middle of the sky, and did not hasten to go down for about a whole day." Critics have pointed out the supposed error of saying that the sun stood still. We know that the earth revolves around the sun, they say, so if an unchanging relationship between the earth and the sun was maintained during the event recorded in Joshua 10, it was the earth that stood still, not the sun. They conclude, therefore, that the Bible is scientifically inaccurate.

But did Joshua intend to make a scientifically precise statement, or was he simply describing a phenomenon? From a human perspective it looked as if the sun stood still. Even the most severe Bible critic may be tempted to describe a beautiful "sunset" or "sunrise." Both those terms are scientifically inaccurate because the sun itself isn't actually rising or setting, though the statements are acceptable descriptions of scientific phenomena.

Such figures of speech are very common. We say that people in Australia live "down under," or we speak of someone's searching "the four corners of the earth." Such expressions are spoken from a human perspective and are not intended to be scientifically accurate. Inspiration does not exclude figures of speech.

(b) Cultural differences

Second Kings 18:14 says that King Hezekiah of Judah paid thirty talents of gold and three hundred talents of silver to Sennacherib, king of Assyria. When archaeologists discovered Sennacherib's record of that transaction they noted that eight hundred talents of silver had been recorded. Critics were quick to point out the supposed inaccuracy of the biblical text. However, further archaeological studies revealed that though the standard of calculating gold was the same in Judea and Syria, the standard of calculating silver was different. It took eight hundred Syrian talents to equal three hundred Hebrew talents (cf. Joseph Free, *Archaeology and Bible History* [Wheaton,

Ill.: Scripture Press, 1950], p. 208). Scripture recorded the Hebrew figures; Sennacherib recorded the Syrian figures.

The Bible is accurate about all truth because God is its author.

E. Its Evidence

1. Science

Although the Bible has been criticized as unscientific, it revealed some of the basic principles of science centuries before scientists understood them.

a) The matrix of existence

Nineteenth century English philosopher Herbert Spencer was famous for applying scientific discoveries to philosophy. He categorized that which is knowable in the natural sciences—the matrix of existence—as time, force, motion, space, and matter. As brilliant as his classifications are, they simply affirm what God revealed millennia ago: "In the beginning [time] God [force] created [motion] the heavens [space] and the earth [matter]" (Gen. 1:1). The matrix of existence is in the first verse of the Bible!

In addition, the universe is a continuum of time, force, motion, space, and matter. Since one element can't exist without the others, the entire continuum must have existed simultaneously from the beginning. That simultaneous beginning is what the Bible calls creation.

b) The first law of thermodynamics

The first law of thermodynamics (the law of conservation of mass and energy) states that the total energy of the universe is constant—all energy and matter are sustained by their interplay.

The Bible teaches that the universe was designed to operate in an orderly fashion. Once the matrix of time, force, motion, space, and matter was generated, no further creation was needed. That's why God ceased from His creative activity after completing His work (Gen. 2:2).

c) The second law of thermodynamics

The second law of thermodynamics is the law of increasing disorder: the matrix of existence is running down and will eventually die. Although the total energy of the universe is constant, it continues to be transformed into lower levels of availability.

Science cannot explain that phenomenon, but the Bible gives a clear explanation: sin brought a curse upon all creation. In fact, creation itself eagerly awaits the day when it will be set free from its slavery to corruption (Rom. 8:19, 21).

The Bible refers to many areas of science, and in each case it is with complete accuracy.

2. Fulfilled prophecy

The fulfilled prophecies against Tyre and Sidon demonstrate the historical accuracy of the Bible.

a) The destruction of Tyre

Ezekiel prophesied the destruction of Tyre, a Phoenician stronghold on the coast of modern-day Lebanon: "The word of the Lord came to me saying, 'Son of man, because Tyre has said concerning Jerusalem, "Aha, the gateway of the peoples is broken; it has opened to me. I shall be filled, now that she is laid waste," therefore, thus says the Lord God, "Behold, I am against you, O Tyre, and I will bring up many nations against you, as the sea brings up its waves. And they will destroy the walls of Tyre and break down her towers; and I will scrape her debris from her and make her a bare rock. She will be a place for the spreading of nets in the midst of the sea, for I have spoken," declares the Lord God, "and she will become spoil for the nations.

"Also her daughters who are on the mainland will be slain by the sword, and they will know that I am the Lord." ' For thus says the Lord God, 'Behold, I will bring upon Tyre from the north Nebuchadnezzar king of Babylon, king of kings, with horses, chariots, cavalry, and a great army. He will slay your daughters on the mainland with the sword; and he will make siege walls against you, cast up a mound against you, and raise up a large shield against you. And the blow of his battering rams he will direct against your walls, and with his axes he will break down your towers.

'Because of the multitude of his horses, the dust raised by them will cover you; your walls will shake at the noise of cavalry and wagons and chariots, when he enters your gates as men enter a city that is breached. With the hoofs of his horses he will trample all your streets. He will slay your people with the sword; and your strong pillars will come down to the ground.

'Also they will make a spoil of your riches and a prey of your merchandise, break down your walls and destroy your pleasant houses, and throw your stones and your timbers and your debris into the water. So I will silence the sound of your songs, and the sound of your harps will be heard no more. I will make you a bare rock; you will be a place for the spreading of nets. You will be built no more, for I the Lord have spoken,' declares the Lord God. Thus says the Lord God to Tyre" (Ezek. 26:1-15).

That is a very specific prophecy against a city that had controlled Phoenicia since the seventh century B.C. The city was well fortified with walls about 150 feet high and 15 feet thick. Hiram I was its most notable king. He is mentioned in the Old Testament as having sent craftsmen to help build David's palace, and cedar to be used in its construction (2 Sam. 5:11); he also supplied cedar and cyprus to Solomon for the construction of the Temple (1 Kings 5:10).

Not long after Ezekiel's prophecy was given, Nebuchadnezzar, king of Babylon, laid a thirteen-year siege to Tyre (586-573 B.C.). His strategy was to cut off anything coming into the city so that the people would eventually starve and be forced to surrender. By the time he breached the walls of the city he realized that the people of Tyre had relocated all their valuables and most of their citizens to a small island a half mile offshore. Although he destroyed the coastal city of Tyre, Nebuchadnezzar had no naval fleet, so he was unable to attack the island city. Consequently, he gained no spoils from his victory (Ezek. 29:18).

Ezekiel's prophecy remained partially fulfilled until about 250 years later when Alexander the Great approached Tyre on his way to Egypt after defeating the Persians. When the people of Tyre refused to open their gates to him, he laid siege to the island.

His strategy was to build a causeway from the mainland to the island by scraping the debris from the old city into the ocean. During the construction of the causeway his men came under heavy attack from projectiles thrown or shot at them by the people of Tyre. To protect his men, Alexander ordered the construction of large shells to be held over them as they worked.

The island city was fortified with powerful walls that reached to the edge of the sea. To scale the walls, Alexander built 160-foot high mobile siege towers that held artillery troops and a drop bridge. The artillery troops shot at the people from the towers as other soldiers slowly pushed the towers along the causeway. When they reached the wall the bridges were lowered, thereby enabling Alexander's army to penetrate the city.

The siege lasted seven months. Alexander's troops killed about eight thousand people and sold thirty thousand into slavery.

The coastal city of Tyre has never been rebuilt, and today it is a place where fishermen dry their nets. Every detail of Ezekiel's prophecy has been fulfilled. The statistician and scientist Peter Stoner calculated the probability of that happening by chance to be one in seventy-five million (*Science Speaks* [Chicago: Moody, 1969], p. 79).

b) The judgment against Sidon

Ezekiel also prophesied against the city of Sidon: "Thus says the Lord God, 'Behold, I am against you, O Sidon, and I shall be glorified in your midst. Then they will know that I am the Lord, when I execute judgments in her, and I shall manifest My holiness in her. For I shall send pestilence to her and blood to her streets, and the wounded will fall in her midst by the sword upon her on every side; then they will know that I am the Lord' " (Ezek. 28:22-23).

Sidon was located some twenty miles north of Tyre and was the center of Baal worship. Ezekiel prophesied bloodshed and violence concerning the city but did not prophesy its ultimate destruction.

The history of Sidon has indeed been marked with bloodshed and violence. In 351 B.C. the people of Sidon rebelled against Persian rule. In the siege that followed forty thousand chose to die rather than to submit to Persian violence, so they set their homes and themselves on fire. Sidon was taken three times by the crusaders and three times by the Moslems. In 1840 it was bombarded by the combined forces of England, France, and Turkey. But despite such devastation, Sidon still exists. It is a seaport in Lebanon.

c) Other prophecies

The Bible is replete with fulfilled prophecies against evil nations: Isaiah 13 predicts the destruction of Babylon; Ezekiel 25, the destruction of Moab and Ammon; Ezekiel 30, the destruction of Egypt; Micah 1, the destruction of Samaria; and Nahum 1, the destruction of Nineveh.

38

Prophecy from a Mathematician's Point of View

Peter Stoner calculated the probability of just eleven Old Testament prophecies occurring by chance to be one in 5.76×10^{59}.

To illustrate the immensity of that number, Professor Stoner said, "Let us round [it] off to 5×10^{59}. Let us suppose that we had that number of silver dollars. . . . It has been estimated that the whole universe contains about two trillion galaxies, each containing about 100 billion stars. From our 5×10^{59} dollars we could make all of the stars, in all of these galaxies, 2×10^{5} times" (pp. 96-97).

Mathematical probability demonstrates the accuracy of the Bible and provides evidence of its divine authorship.

F. Its Benefit

Not only is the Bible the Word of God, but it is also the instrument by which He equips us for every good work. Paul said, "All Scripture is inspired by God and profitable for teaching, for reproof, for correction, for training in righteousness; that the man of God may be adequate, equipped for every good work" (2 Tim. 3:16-17). What a tremendous thing: we have a life-changing Word from God!

Conclusion

God's Word is inspired, accurate, and life-changing. What should be our response to such a precious gift? We must believe it, study it, honor it, love it, obey it, fight for it, and preach it. It is revelation from the living God to His creation.

Focusing on the Facts

1. God communicated His Word through _____ and _____ (see p. 24).
2. Define revelation (see pp. 24-25).
3. How did God reveal Himself in the Old Testament? in the New Testament (see p. 25)?

4. What is the origin of inspiration (see p. 26)?
5. Explain the process of inspiration (see p. 26).
6. How does Jeremiah's call to the ministry illustrate the process of inspiration (Jer. 1:4-6; see p. 27)?
7. What is the extent of inspiration (see p. 27)?
8. Is it accurate to say that the early church invented the canon of Scripture (see p. 27)? Explain.
9. Respond to the view that Scripture is merely the product of human genius (see pp. 28-29).
10. How did the New Testament writers affirm the inspiration and authority of the Old Testament (see p. 29)?
11. Why is it incorrect to say that the Bible contains inspired thoughts but not inspired words (see pp. 30-32)?
12. How is the first law of thermodynamics presented in the Bible (Gen. 2:2; see pp. 34-35)?
13. Explain the second law of thermodynamics (see p. 35). What explanation does the Bible give for that law (Rom. 8:19, 21; see p. 35)?
14. The prophecies against Tyre and Sidon demonstrate the _____ of the Bible (see p. 35).
15. Who were the two rulers who laid siege to Tyre (see p. 37)?
16. How did Peter Stoner use mathematics to demonstrate the accuracy of the Bible (see p. 39)?
17. What is the benefit of having an inspired Bible (2 Tim. 3:16-17; see p. 39)?

Pondering the Principles

1. Paul thanked God for the Thessalonian believers, who "received . . . the word of God's message, [and] accepted it not as the word of men, but for what it really is, the word of God" (1 Thess. 2:13). The impact of the Word on their lives was demonstrated when they "turned to God from idols to serve a living and true God" (1 Thess. 1:9). Is your life characterized by obedience to God's Word? It's one thing to affirm that it is inspired; it's another thing to submit to its authority. Be diligent to spend time each day in prayer and Bible study. Allow God's Spirit to apply His Word to your heart. Don't deny in deed what you affirm in doctrine.

2. David wrote, "O how I love Thy law! It is my meditation all the day" (Ps. 119:97). He understood the benefits to be gained from

studying God's Word, and chronicled many of them in Psalm 119. Read that psalm and make a list of those benefits mentioned. Throughout the coming week select a few each day to meditate upon, and praise God for them.

3. Inspiration extends to every word of Scripture, so every word is important. Have you learned how to study the Bible in such a way that you understand and apply the meaning of its words? It's wonderful to have good Bible teachers to guide our learning, but Paul's admonition to Timothy applies to all believers: "Be diligent to present yourself approved to God as a workman who does not need to be ashamed, handling accurately the word of truth" (2 Tim. 2:15). Consult your church library or local Christian bookstore for books on basic Bible study methods.

3
The Work of the Word—Part 1

Outline

Introduction
A. The Power of God's Word
B. The Priority of God's Word
C. The Promises of God's Word
   1. It is productive
   2. It is swift
   3. It is nourishing

Lesson
I. Salvation (v. 15)
  A. The Testimony of Jesus
    1. John 5:24
    2. John 6:63-64
    3. John 12:49-50
    4. John 20:31
    5. Luke 8:5-15
  B. The Testimony of Paul
    1. Romans 10:13-15, 17
    2. Ephesians 5:25-26
    3. 1 Thessalonians 2:13
  C. The Testimony of James
  D. The Testimony of Nehemiah
  E. The Testimony of Peter
  F. The Testimony of Lydia
II. Teaching (v. 16*a*)
  A. The Definition of Teaching
  B. The Recipients of Teaching

C. The Importance of Teaching
    1. The source of truth
        a) 1 Timothy 6:20
        b) Acts 20:27, 31
        c) John 17:17
    2. The source of knowledge
    3. The source of victory
        a) The armor of God
        b) The temptation of Jesus
D. The Response to Teaching
    1. Obey it
    2. Proclaim it
        a) Matthew 28:19-20
        b) Matthew 22:16

Conclusion

Introduction

A. The Power of God's Word

God's Word has the power to do a supernatural work in our lives. Paul told Timothy, "From childhood you have known the sacred writings which are able to give you the wisdom that leads to salvation through faith which is in Christ Jesus. All Scripture is inspired by God and profitable for teaching, for reproof, for correction, for training in righteousness; that the man of God may be adequate, equipped for every good work" (2 Tim. 3:15-17). Paul's statement delineates the work of the Word in five ways: salvation, teaching, reproof, correction, and training in righteousness.

B. The Priority of God's Word

There are many things a church can do and many priorities it can uphold. But only God's Word, empowered by His Spirit, transforms lives. Therefore, the church must have a strong commitment to biblical authority and expository preaching. We must faithfully teach, preach, exalt, and live God's Word. It must be the focal point of everything we do. When God speaks, we must listen. We must be those who have "an ear . . . [to] hear what the Spirit says to the churches" (Rev. 2:7, 11, 17, 29; 3:6, 13, 22).

C. The Promises of God's Word

1. It is productive

Isaiah said, "As the rain and the snow come down from heaven, and do not return there without watering the earth, and making it bear and sprout, and furnishing seed to the sower and bread to the eater; so shall My word be which goes forth from My mouth; it shall not return to Me empty, without accomplishing what I desire, and without succeeding in the matter for which I send it" (Isa. 55:10-11).

2. It is swift

The Word of God is depicted in Psalm 147 as a swift messenger that runs to do God's work: "He sends forth His command to the earth; His word runs very swiftly. He gives snow like wool; He scatters the frost like ashes. He casts forth His ice as fragments; who can stand before His cold? He sends forth His Word and melts them; He causes His wind to blow and the waters to flow. He declares His words to Jacob, His statutes and His ordinances to Israel" (vv. 15-19).

Just as God sends all the natural elements to produce His desired results, so He sends His Word. And the Word always accomplishes its purpose. That should give tremendous confidence to all who proclaim God's Word.

3. It is nourishing

Deuteronomy 8:3 says that every word out of God's mouth is spiritually nourishing—it feeds believers and causes growth.

God's Word is productive, swift, and nourishing. It accomplishes His work in the lives of His people. That work begins with salvation.

Lesson

I. SALVATION (v. 15)

"From childhood you have known the sacred writings which are able to give you the wisdom that leads to salvation through faith which is in Christ Jesus."

Paul was acknowledging that his disciple Timothy had had a godly upbringing from his mother, Eunice, and grandmother, Lois (2 Tim. 1:5).

The Greek word translated "sacred writings" refers in this context to the Old Testament; however, both the Old and New Testaments are the instruments of salvation. That truth is affirmed throughout the Bible.

A. The Testimony of Jesus

1. John 5:24

Jesus said, "Truly, truly, I say to you, he who hears My word, and believes Him who sent Me, has eternal life, and does not come into judgment, but has passed out of death into life." That tremendous verse gives the essence of the gospel: hearing Christ's Word and believing in God.

2. John 6:63-64

Jesus said to His followers, "It is the Spirit who gives life; the flesh profits nothing; the words that I have spoken to you are spirit and are life. But there are some of you who do not believe." The Word is the agent of salvation, but it must be mixed with faith to produce eternal life.

3. John 12:49-50

Jesus said, "I did not speak on My own initiative, but the Father Himself who sent Me has given Me commandment, what to say, and what to speak. And I know that His commandment is eternal life; therefore the things I speak, I speak just as the Father has told Me." Jesus spoke only the Word of God, and He understood its power to produce eternal life.

4. John 20:31

John affirmed the fact that eternal life comes by believing the Word of God; that's why he wrote his gospel. He said, "These have been written that you may believe that Jesus is the Christ, the Son of God; and that believing you may have life in His name."

5. Luke 8:5-15

Jesus told the parable of the sower to illustrate the kind of person who is receptive to God's Word: " 'The sower went out to sow his seed; and as he sowed, some fell beside the road; and it was trampled under foot, and the birds of the air ate it up. And other seed fell on rocky soil, and as soon as it grew up, it withered away, because it had no moisture. And other seed fell among the thorns; and the thorns grew up with it, and choked it out. And other seed fell into the good soil, and grew up, and produced a crop a hundred times as great.' As He said these things, He would call out, 'He who has ears to hear, let him hear' " (vv. 5-8).

When His disciples asked for an explanation of His parable, Jesus replied, "To you it has been granted to know the mysteries of the kingdom of God, but to the rest it is in parables, in order that seeing they may not see, and hearing they may not understand" (v. 10). His parables brought understanding to believers but were riddles to unbelievers.

Jesus explained, "The seed is the word of God" (v. 11). That's the point: the Word of God produces new life in a receptive heart, but if a heart isn't receptive there will be no product.

He continued, "Those beside the road are those who have heard; then the devil comes and takes away the word from their heart, so that they may not believe and be saved. And those on the rocky soil are those who, when they hear, receive the word with joy; and these have no firm root; they believe for a while, and in time of temptation fall away. And the seed which fell among the thorns, these are the ones who have heard, and as they go on their way they are choked with worries and riches and pleasures of this life, and bring no fruit to maturity. And the seed in the good soil, these are the ones who have heard the word in an honest and good heart, and hold it fast, and bear fruit with perseverance" (vv. 12-15).

God's Word produces salvation in a receptive heart.

B. The Testimony of Paul

1. Romans 10:13-15, 17

Paul said, "Faith comes from hearing, and hearing by the word of Christ" (v. 17). Faith comes from hearing the Word—that's why preachers are so important. In verses 13-15 Paul says, "Whoever will call upon the name of the Lord will be saved. How then shall they call upon Him in whom they have not believed? And how shall they believe in Him whom they have not heard? And how shall they hear without a preacher? And how shall they preach unless they are sent?" And when they are sent they must preach the Word of Christ, which is the source of salvation.

2. Ephesians 5:25-26

In comparing marriage with the church, Paul said, "Husbands, love your wives, just as Christ also loved the church and gave Himself up for her; that He might sanctify her, having cleansed her by the washing of water with the word." Christ has saved and cleansed His church through the agency of His Word.

3. 1 Thessalonians 2:13

Paul said, "The word of God . . . performs its work in you who believe." The Word does its work in a believing heart.

C. The Testimony of James

James refers to the same dynamic in James 1:18: "He brought us forth by the word of truth." "Brought us forth" in this context means "to beget," "redeem," or "save." God saved us by the Word of truth.

D. The Testimony of Nehemiah

Nehemiah 8 tells of the beginning of a revival in Israel after the Babylonian Captivity. The chapter begins, "All the people gathered as one man at the square which is in front of the Water Gate, and they asked Ezra the scribe to bring the book of the law of Moses which the Lord had given to Israel. Then Ezra the priest brought the law before the assembly of men, women, and all who could listen with understanding, on the first day of the seventh month. And he read from it before the square which was in front of the Water Gate from early morning until midday, in the presence of men and women, those who could understand; and all the people were attentive to the book of the law" (vv. 1-3).

The people stood and listened for hour after hour while "Ezra . . . stood at a wooden podium which they had made for the purpose. . . . And Ezra opened the book in the sight of all the people for he was standing above all the people; and when he opened it, all the people stood up. Then Ezra blessed the Lord the great God. And all the people answered, 'Amen, Amen!' while lifting up their hands; then they bowed low and worshiped the Lord with their faces to the ground. . . . And they read from the book, from the law of God, translating to give the sense so that they understood the reading" (vv. 4-6, 8).

It was necessary to translate the Hebrew text into the more common Aramaic language, then to explain its meaning. Ezra and the scribes were reading, translating, and explaining the Word.

The people's response was amazing: "All the people were weeping when they heard the words of the law" (v. 9). They were grieved over their sin and turned back to God.

Verse 18 says that Ezra "read from the book of the law of God daily, from the first day to the last day. And they celebrated the feast seven days, and on the eighth day there was a solemn assembly according to the ordinance."

In chapter 9 the people began to praise the God who had revealed Himself in Scripture. In 10:29 it says that all the people joined together and took "on themselves a curse and an oath to walk in God's law . . . and to keep and to observe all the commandments of God [their] Lord, and His ordinances and His statutes."

That was a great revival, and I believe that throughout that seven-day feast many were saved. It was a direct result of the people's hearing and understanding Scripture.

The Role of God's Word in Evangelism

Sometimes people say to me, "If you teach the Bible all the time, when do you evangelize?" I simply explain that the Bible is the greatest tool for evangelism. When I preach or teach the Word I *am* evangelizing.

When a lawyer asked Jesus, "What shall I do to inherit eternal life?" Jesus directed him to Scripture: "What is written in the Law? How does it read to you?" (Luke 10:25-26). In John 5:39 Jesus says, "Search the Scriptures . . . it is these that bear witness of Me." The Scriptures are able to give us the wisdom that leads to salvation (2 Tim. 3:15). Therefore, the heart and soul of our evangelistic ministry must be the faithful proclamation of God's Word.

E. The Testimony of Peter

First Peter 1:23 says, "You have been born again not of seed which is perishable but imperishable, that is, through the living and abiding word of God." God's Word is the seed that produces salvation.

The implications of that verse are profound yet practical. If you want to be effective in evangelism you must present God's Word. Evangelism needn't be as complicated as we sometimes make it. We don't have to explain every theological issue or answer every question; the main thing is to be faithful proclaimers of God's Word. It can be as simple as giving an unsaved friend a Bible and encouraging him to read the gospels. God will prepare the soil; we must plant the seed.

Peter then went on to say, "This is the word which was preached to you" (v. 25). He illustrated his point by comparing the Word of God to flesh: the Word abides forever and produces spiritual life, but all flesh is temporary and eventually fades like grass (vv. 24-25; cf. Isa. 40:6-8).

F. The Testimony of Lydia

Acts 16:14 records the account of Lydia's conversion: "A certain woman named Lydia, from the city of Thyatira, a seller of purple fabrics, a worshiper of God, was listening; and the Lord opened her heart to respond to the things spoken by Paul." Lydia worshiped the true God but had not yet heard the gospel of Christ. The Lord graciously opened her heart to receive the preaching of Paul.

That's the essence of evangelism. We proclaim the gospel, and God opens hearts.

So Scripture is the source of salvation. That's why Paul called it "the word of life" (Phil. 2:16). As the psalmist said, "The law of the Lord is perfect, converting the soul" (Ps. 19:7, KJV).

II. TEACHING (v. 16a)

A. The Definition of Teaching

The word translated "teaching" (Gk., *didaskalia*) refers in this passage to the content of teaching rather than to the process of teaching. The point is that Scripture gives us a body of doctrinal truth to govern our thoughts and actions.

B. The Recipients of Teaching

Biblical doctrine is most productive in the hearts of believers because "a natural man does not accept the things of the Spirit of God; for they are foolishness to him, and he cannot understand them, because they are spiritually appraised" (1 Cor. 2:14).

Believers have the illuminating ministry of the Holy Spirit to give them understanding of God's Word—they have "the mind of Christ" (1 Cor. 2:16). John said to his Christian audience, "The anointing which you have received from Him abides in you, and you have no need for anyone to teach you; but . . . His anointing teaches you about all things" (1 John 2:27).

C. The Importance of Teaching

1. The source of truth

A primary purpose of Scripture is to provide believers with a repository of divine truth—principles for life and thought.

The Relation of Biblical Truth to Holy Living

The depth of our holiness is directly proportional to our knowledge of God's Word. The Holy Spirit empowers us to apply biblical principles to our lives, but we must first study God's Word and saturate our minds with its truth. We can't function on principles we don't understand.

The driving force in my own ministry has always been an insatiable desire to know what God's Word means and to impart that knowledge to others. That desire is what compels me to study long hours. I don't want any gaps in my understanding of God's Word.

Over the years many people have told me that they could have avoided some difficult situations if their knowledge of Scripture had been more complete. Perhaps you can identify with that common problem. Gaining an understanding of God's Word guards us and guides us through life. Even though that learning process takes a long time, God has simplified it by repeating biblical principles throughout Scripture and illustrating them in a myriad of ways. We must patiently and thoroughly pursue that sacred knowledge.

a) 1 Timothy 6:20—Paul said to Timothy, "Guard what has been entrusted to you." Paul viewed apostolic doctrine as a body of truth that he was to entrust faithfully to others.

b) Acts 20:27, 31—Paul told the Ephesian elders, "I did not shrink from declaring to you the whole purpose of God. . . . Night and day for a period of three years I did not cease to admonish each one with tears." He faithfully taught God's Word so that those people would have a body of divine truth by which to govern their lives.

c) John 17:17—Jesus said to the Father, "Thy word is truth." Nothing is more important in life than knowing the truth.

2. The source of knowledge

The Lord says in Hosea 4:6, "My people are destroyed for lack of knowledge." They had rejected true knowledge, so they were unable to live lives that were pleasing to God.

God's Word is the source of truth and knowledge. Therefore, believers must be exposed to the faithful, systematic proclamation of God's truth so that they can know its principles and learn to apply them to their lives.

3. The source of victory

a) The armor of God

In Ephesians 6 Paul presents a vivid illustration of the importance of God's Word to the believer. To gain victory against the forces of Satan (v. 12) one must put on the full armor of God, which consists of the belt of truth, the breastplate of righteousness, the shoes of the gospel of peace, the shield of faith, the helmet of salvation, and the sword of the Spirit (vv. 13-17).

The only offensive weapon is the sword of the Spirit —the Word of God (v. 17). The Greek word translated "sword" is not *rhomphaia*, which refers to a broadsword, but *machaira*, which refers to a small six-inch dagger. The Greek word translated "word" (*rhēma*) refers to a specific statement. The Word of God is to be used skillfully and precisely by applying a specific statement of Scripture to a specific temptation, as a small dagger would be applied with great dexterity to a vital area. Having access to a Bible is not the issue. Spiritual warfare requires precise knowledge and application of biblical truth.

Accurate Interpretation Comes Before Effective Application

Before we can apply Scripture effectively, we must interpret it accurately. That's why Paul told Timothy, "Be diligent to present yourself approved to God as a workman who does not need to be ashamed, handling accurately the word of truth" (2 Tim. 2:15).

As a pastor/teacher, my responsibility is to study God's Word thoroughly and teach it with accuracy and clarity so that God's people are better equipped to be victorious in spiritual battle. Their responsibility is to master the Word so that they can use it with precision.

How effective is your spiritual armor? Do you have a thorough grasp of the sword of the Spirit?

b) The temptation of Jesus

The best example of an effective application of God's Word was given by Jesus in Matthew 4:1-11. Each time the devil tempted Him He responded by quoting a verse from Deuteronomy that was a direct rebuttal. He didn't have to quote Scripture; He could have said anything and it would have become Scripture. But by quoting Scripture He left us with an example of how to deal with temptation. He used the sword with precision to strike a fatal blow. That's what we're to do.

D. The Response to Teaching

1. Obey it

Exodus 24:7 says that Moses "took the book of the covenant and read it in the hearing of the people; and they
said, 'All that the Lord has spoken we will do, and we
will be obedient!' " That ought to be our commitment,
too. We should desire to know and obey all that God
has said.

2. Proclaim it

a) Matthew 28:19-20—The disciples were told to "go
. . . and make disciples of all the nations, baptizing
them . . . [and] teaching them to observe all that [Je-
sus] commanded." The responsibility to teach divine
truth extends to us as well.

b) Matthew 22:16—When some of the Pharisees and
Herodians came to Jesus to try to catch Him in His
own words, they began by saying, "Teacher, we
know that You are truthful and teach the way of God
in truth, and defer to no one; for You are not partial
to any." That statement may be one of the most wonderful commendations ever given to Jesus by unbelievers. They knew He was committed to truth and
couldn't be intimidated. He taught with integrity and
impartiality because people needed to hear God's
Word.

Many today are more concerned about not offending
their listeners than they are about proclaiming biblical truth. Though it isn't necessary to browbeat people, we must speak the truth with love and without
compromise. Some people will be offended when the
gospel confronts their sin, but that's what it's supposed to do. Remember the example of Jesus, who
didn't defer to anyone as a consequence of fear of offending them.

Paul felt the same way. In Acts 20:24 he says, "I do
not consider my life of any account as dear to myself,

in order that I may finish my course, and the ministry which I received from the Lord Jesus, to testify solemnly of the gospel of the grace of God." He had a mission to accomplish and did so with integrity.

Are You Committed to Biblical Truth?

We must be committed to biblical truth because it establishes divine parameters for our behavior in every area of life. King Josiah had such a commitment. Second Chronicles 34:31 says that he "stood in his place and made a covenant before the Lord to walk after the Lord, to keep His commandments and His testimonies and His statutes with all his heart and with all his soul, to perform the words of the covenant written in this book." What a devoted man!

God is calling people to commit themselves to His Word. The practical implications of such a commitment are obvious: first we must know His Word, then we must live it.

I have an old Bible that sits by the entrance to our home. It is opened to Joshua 1:7-8: "Be strong and very courageous; be careful to do according to all the law which Moses My servant commanded you; do not turn from it to the right or to the left, so that you may have success wherever you go. This book of the law shall not depart from your mouth, but you shall meditate on it day and night, so that you may be careful to do according to all that is written in it; for then you will make your way prosperous, and then you will have success."

Every time I enter or leave my home I am reminded to do all that is written in Scripture, and that is my commitment. It is yours? Do you recognize God's Word as the only source of true doctrine? There are commentaries and books that help us understand the Bible, but remember—the Bible itself is the source of divine truth. Do you study it and prayerfully apply it to your life?

Conclusion

So the Word of God is profitable for salvation and teaching. God wants us to be exposed to it constantly and systematically so that the Word of Christ might richly dwell within us (Col. 3:16)—nourishing, saturating, and renewing our minds. That will enable us to act and think in accordance with His truth.

That is the work of the Word, and it always accomplishes its work in a believing heart. I trust yours is that kind of heart.

Focusing on the Facts

1. What five works of the Word are delineated in 2 Timothy 3:15-17 (see p. 44)?
2. What must the church have (see p. 44)?
3. How is God's Word depicted in Psalm 147:15-19 (see p. 45)?
4. According to John 5:24, what is the essence of the gospel (see p. 46)?
5. The Word is the agent of salvation, but it must be mixed with _____ life (see p. 46).
6. Why did John write his gospel (John 20:31; see p. 47)?
7. In the parable of the sower, what is the seed (Luke 8:11; see p. 47)?
8. In the parable of the sower, what type of person is represented by the good soil (Luke 8:15; see p. 48)?
9. By what means did Christ save and cleanse His church (Eph. 5:26; see p. 48)?
10. What was the response of the people in Nehemiah 8:9 to the preaching of God's Word (see p. 49)?
11. What is the role of God's Word in evangelism (see p. 50)?
12. God's Word is the _____ that produces _____ (1 Pet. 1:23; see p. 50).
13. What does "teaching" in 2 Timothy 3:16 refer to (see p. 51)?
14. What is a primary purpose of Scripture (see p. 52)?
15. Explain the relation of biblical truth to holy living (see p. 52).
16. What type of sword does Ephesians 6:17 refer to, and how does that type of sword illustrate the proper usage of God's Word (see p. 54)?
17. What is the relationship between the interpretation and the application of Scripture (see p. 54)?
18. What example did Jesus give us in Matthew 4:1-11 (see p. 54)?
19. What important commitment did King Josiah make in 2 Chronicles 34:31 (see p. 56)?

Pondering the Principles

1. We have seen that the faithful proclamation of God's Word is essential to effective evangelism. Perhaps you have been praying for an unbeliever, but you've not yet communicated the gospel to him or her. Pray that God will give you the opportunity and boldness to do so, and be sure to take advantage of that opportunity as soon as it comes along.

2. Bible study is an absolute necessity for the Christian, but it can be fruitless if you're not willing to obey what you learn. King Josiah made a very significant commitment to God when he vowed to "keep His commandments . . . testimonies and . . . statutes with all his heart and . . . soul" (2 Chron. 34:31). That is the commitment of a true believer. Does Josiah's commitment reflect your desire? John said, "The one who says, 'I have come to know Him,' and does not keep His commandments, is a liar, and the truth is not in him; but whoever keeps His word, in him the love of God has truly been perfected. By this we know that we are in Him: the one who says he abides in Him ought himself to walk in the same manner as He walked" (1 John 2:4-6). Let your commitment to God's Word reflect the genuineness of your faith.

3. God has entrusted His Word to every believer. Each of us has the responsibility to learn and apply it, then to impart what we have learned to others (Matt. 28:20; 2 Tim. 2:2). No matter how much or how little you know, there is always someone who can benefit from what you've learned. Are you aware of such a person in your life? If so, be faithful to encourage that person in his or her biblical studies. If not, pray that God will direct you to someone soon so that you can experience the great joy of nurturing one of God's children.

4
The Work of the Word—Part 2

Outline

Introduction
A. The Defense of Scripture
B. The Sufficiency of Scripture

Review
I. Salvation (v. 15)
II. Teaching (v. 16a)

Lesson
III. Reproof (v. 16b)
  A. Defined
  B. Delineated
    1. Reproving sinful conduct
      a) 2 Timothy 4:2
      b) Hebrews 4:12-13
    2. Reproving erroneous teaching
      a) Psalm 119:99-100, 104
      b) Isaiah 8:19-20
      c) 2 Peter 3:16
IV. Correction (v. 16c)
  A. Defined
  B. Described
    1. Psalm 119:11
    2. John 15:1-3
    3. Galatians 6:1
V. Training (v. 16d)
  A. Defined
  B. Demonstrated

1. Hebrews 12:5-11
2. Acts 20:32
3. 1 Timothy 4:6
4. Matthew 4:4
5. 1 Peter 1:23; 2:2
6. Psalm 19:7-9

Conclusion

Introduction

In 2 Timothy 3:15-16 Paul says to Timothy, "From childhood you have known the sacred writings which are able to give you the wisdom that leads to salvation through faith which is in Christ Jesus. All Scripture is inspired by God and profitable for teaching, for reproof, for correction, for training in righteousness; that the man of God may be adequate, equipped for every good work."

That is the most concise statement in the New Testament regarding the work of God's Word in our lives. It produces salvation (v. 15); it teaches, reproves, corrects, and trains (v. 16); and it equips us for all that God requires of us (v. 17). In short, it is sufficient for every aspect of spiritual life (cf. Ps. 19:7-11 and Ps. 119).

A. The Defense of Scripture

The sufficiency and authority of Scripture is constantly under attack by false religious systems that attempt to distort or add to its message. That's why Jude admonished his readers to "contend earnestly for the faith which was once for all delivered to the saints" (Jude 3).

We must earnestly defend biblical truth. One way to do that is to demonstrate its truthfulness. Paul said, "All Scripture is inspired by God" (v. 16). That is a profound statement about the source and truth of Scripture. It is not the word of man; it is the Word of God. As such it is inspired, sufficient, authoritative, and true.

B. The Sufficiency of Scripture

Regarding our spiritual life and our relationship with God, the Bible is all that is necessary for proper instruction to equip us for godliness. That's why I am committed to the systematic teaching of God's Word. I want God's people to experience its transforming power in their lives.

A Severe Warning

God will not tolerate anyone's tampering with or distorting His Word in any way. Any attempt to do so will result in severe judgment. The apostle John said, "If anyone adds to [the book of Revelation], God shall add to him the plagues which are written in this book; and if anyone takes away from the words of the book of this prophecy, God shall take away his part from the tree of life and from the holy city" (Rev. 22:18-19). That's a severe warning.

Review

I. SALVATION (v. 15) (see pp. 46-51)

God's Word empowered by His Spirit has the ability to save, so we must be committed to proclaiming it to unbelievers.

II. TEACHING (v. 16a) (see pp. 51-56)

Scripture guides us in every aspect of life, so we must pursue a thorough knowledge of it.

Lesson

III. REPROOF (v. 16b)

A. Defined

In its strictest sense the Greek word translated "reproof" (*elegmos*) means "to rebuke" or "to confront someone regarding misconduct or false teaching." That is the negative aspect: God's Word lays the foundation of doctrinal truth but also rebukes everything opposed to it.

B. Delineated

There are two aspects of reproof illustrated in Scripture.

1. Reproving sinful conduct

   a) 2 Timothy 4:2

   Paul instructed Timothy to "preach the word; be ready in season and out of season; reprove, rebuke, exhort." That's a negative ministry in a sense—calling people back from error. The Word of God has that effect.

   In commenting on the meaning of "reproof," Archbishop Richard Trench said, "It is so to rebuke another, with such effectual wielding of the victorious arm of the truth, as to bring him, if not always to a confession, yet at least to a conviction, of his sin" (*Synonyms of the New Testament* [Grand Rapids: Eerdmans, 1983], p. 13). As you study God's Word it convicts you of your sin.

   b) Hebrews 4:12-13

   The writer of Hebrews pictured God's Word as a weapon: "the Word of God is living and active and sharper than any two-edged sword, and piercing as far as the division of soul and spirit, of both joints and marrow, and able to judge the thoughts and intentions of the heart" (v. 12). That's a vivid picture of the power of the Word penetrating the very core of a person's being, just as a huge broadsword penetrates a person's flesh. The Word cuts deeply, exposing and judging our innermost thoughts and motives.

   Perhaps you've had the experience of going to church feeling pretty good about yourself but coming away feeling terrible because God's Word penetrated your heart and revealed your sin. That's why it's so important for the church faithfully to proclaim God's Word. God's Word convicts God's people of their sin. It also insures that the church will not become a haven for complacent sinners. Who wants to be placed under conviction week after week unless he is committed to repentance and obedience? Jesus said, "Everyone who does evil hates the light, and does not come to the light, lest his deeds should be exposed" (John 3:20). Hardened sinners will avoid or oppose the cutting power of God's Word.

Sometimes believers do so as well. If you find yourself avoiding other believers, church services, or Bible study, it may be because you're harboring sin that you don't want exposed. At that point you need to "test yourselves to see if you are in the faith; examine yourselves!" (2 Cor. 13:5).

Hebrews 4:13 says, "There is no creature hidden from His sight, but all things are open and laid bare to the eyes of Him with whom we have to do." God uses His Word to cut deep into your heart, laying you open before His eyes. Commentator William Barclay tells us that the Greek word translated "laid bare" was used among soldiers to describe a criminal who was being led to judgment or execution. Often a soldier would hold the point of a dagger under the criminal's chin, forcing him to hold his head high so everyone could see who he was (*The Letter to the Hebrews* [Philadelphia: Westminster, 1976], p. 40).

A Bittersweet Experience in God's Word

There's a certain amount of shame and guilt associated with lawlessness. Perhaps you have seen a criminal on television who covered his face with his hands or ducked under his coat to avoid the cameras. God's Word does not allow us to hide from His view. It lays us bare—forces us to face God, who sees us as we are. There's no way to hide. The Word exposes our attitudes and thoughts, and it convicts us of our sin.

Every believer experiences the reproving work of the Word. For example, you may be studying a passage of Scripture that speaks of God's love and realize you are lacking in love for God and for others. Or you may be reading about bitterness, hatred, or pride and realize you are harboring such sins in your heart. That's the cutting, convicting work of God's Word, and we should thank Him for it. In fact, we should be as eager to be reproved by the Word as we are to be instructed by it. Why? Because if we're truly God's children, we will hunger for His righteousness (Matt. 5:6). And righteousness will come as our sin is exposed, we see it for what it is, and we confess it. That's a bittersweet experience, but its result is greater holiness.

2. Reproving erroneous teaching

Not only does the Word reprove sin, but it also reproves and exposes false teaching. If you have a thorough knowledge of Scripture, you can easily recognize false teaching because Scripture is the standard by which all teaching must be measured. Whatever claims to be truth must conform to God's Word. That's why so many false religions attempt to add to Scripture or distort its meaning. They have to alter the standard to justify their errors. They are guilty of "peddling" (2 Cor. 2:17) and "adulterating" (2 Cor. 4:2) the Word of God. They do not properly teach and affirm it.

a) Psalm 119:99-100, 104

All 176 verses of Psalm 119 are dedicated to God's Word. The writer says, "I have more insight than all my teachers, for Thy testimonies are my meditation. I understand more than the aged, because I have observed Thy precepts. . . . From Thy precepts I get understanding; therefore I hate every false way." As we gain understanding from God's Word we are able to recognize and avoid false teaching and sinful behavior.

b) Isaiah 8:19-20

Isaiah said, "When they say to you, 'Consult the mediums and the spiritists who whisper and mutter,' shall not a people consult their God? Should they consult the dead on behalf of the living?" (v. 19) Instead of consulting the Bible, many people today turn to mediums and spiritists who supposedly contact the dead or claim to dispense information about the unknown. Such activity is not new; it was present in Old Testament times—even among God's people. But Isaiah said, "To the law and to the testimony! If they do not speak according to this word, it is because they have no dawn" (v. 20). Mediums and spiritists are in spiritual darkness—they have nothing of value to say. Everything God wants us to know is revealed in His Word.

How to Be Noble-Minded

Acts 17:11 describes a very special group of people: the Bereans, who "were more noble-minded than those in Thessalonica, for they received the word with great eagerness, examining the Scriptures daily, to see whether these things [what Paul and Silas were teaching] were so." They exercised discernment in receiving any teaching that claimed to be from God. They didn't want to be "carried about by every wind of doctrine, by the trickery of men, by craftiness in deceitful scheming" (Eph. 4:14). God's Word was their standard, and it must be ours as well. We must affirm its truthfulness and diligently learn its truth.

    c) 2 Peter 3:16

        We must avoid those who "distort . . . the Scriptures, to their own destruction."

The Word of God has the positive ministry of imparting truth (teaching), and the negative ministry of exposing sin and error (reproof). Those works of the Word relate to content. The two remaining works (correction and training) relate to conduct.

IV. CORRECTION (v. 16c)

A. Defined

Scripture not only exposes sin and error but also has the ability to correct both. The Greek word translated "correction" (*epanorthōsis*) appears only here in the New Testament and literally means "to straighten up" or "to lift up." The idea is that God's Word can restore us to a proper spiritual posture.

B. Described

Correction is a wonderful work of the Word. It occurs when you read Scripture and feel conviction as it pierces your heart. I rarely read Scripture without feeling convicted. But it also gives me instruction to build me up again.

I believe with all my heart that our weaknesses can become areas of great strength as we allow God's Word to "richly dwell within [us]" (Col. 3:16). It has the power to build us up (Acts 20:32); it puts the pieces back together.

1. Psalm 119:11

David said, "Thy word I have treasured in my heart, that I may not sin against Thee." The Word builds spiritual strength.

2. John 15:1-3

Jesus said, "I am the true vine, and My Father is the vinedresser. Every branch in Me that does not bear fruit, He takes away; and every branch that bears fruit, He prunes it, that it may bear more fruit. You are already clean because of the word which I have spoken to you."

Jesus compared the believer to a branch that develops excess branches which sap its energy and restrict its fruitfulness. The Father uses the Word (v. 3) to prune away the excess branches, thus promoting growth and productivity. The Word exposes our sin, then shows us the path of obedience. That's the tremendous restoring ministry of God's Word.

3. Galatians 6:1

Paul said, "If a man is caught in any trespass, you who are spiritual, restore such a one in a spirit of gentleness." Whether it comes through private study or through one Christian gently confronting another, God's Word has the ability to draw the sinner back to Christ.

God's Promise of Restoration

God's Word will rebuild and restore the repentant sinner. We need not despair. Job said, "The righteous shall hold to his way, and he who has clean hands shall grow stronger and stronger" (Job 17:9). As your sin is exposed and confessed you are rebuilt, and you become increasingly strengthened through that process. That's the correcting work of the Word.

From the standpoint of content, the Word provides teaching and reproof of sin and error. From the standpoint of conduct, it rebuilds and restores the repentant sinner.

V. TRAINING (v. 16*d*)

A. Defined

"Training in righteousness" is the positive side of correction. The Word corrects you by dealing with your sin; it trains you by providing righteous input. The Greek word translated "training" (*paidion*) is related to the word for "children" (*paideia*). It refers to training or educating a child. It is also used in the New Testament to speak of chastening. God's Word is able to nurture you and bring you to maturity.

B. Demonstrated

1. Hebrews 12:5-11

Verses 5-6 say, "You have forgotten the exhortation which is addressed to you as sons, 'My son, do not regard lightly the discipline [training process] of the Lord, nor faint when you are reproved by Him; for those whom the Lord loves He disciplines, and He scourges every son whom He receives.' " Reproof and scourging are part of the training process, but the term "training" emphasizes the positive aspect of that process.

Verses 7-11 say, "It is for discipline that you endure; God deals with you as with sons; for what son is there whom his father does not discipline? But if you are without discipline, of which all have become partakers, then you are illegitimate children and not sons. Furthermore, we had earthly fathers to discipline us, and we respected them; shall we not much rather be subject to the Father of spirits, and live? For they disciplined us for a short time as seemed best to them, but He disciplines us for our good, that we may share His holiness. And all discipline for the moment seems not to be joyful, but sorrowful; yet to those who have been trained by it, afterwards it yields the peaceful fruit of righteousness."

God puts each of His children through a training process so that each will yield the fruit of righteousness. He uses the Word to provide true doctrine, expose and correct sin, and instruct in righteousness.

2. Acts 20:32

Paul said, "I commend you to God and to the word of His grace, which is able to build you up and to give you the inheritance among all those who are sanctified." God's Word edifies, strengthens, and encourages believers.

3. 1 Timothy 4:6

Paul instructed Timothy to be "constantly nourished on the words of the faith and of . . . sound doctrine." The Word nourishes and builds us up.

4. Matthew 4:4

Jesus said, "Man shall not live on bread alone, but on every word that proceeds out of the mouth of God." God's Word is our spiritual food.

5. 1 Peter 1:23; 2:2

Peter said, "You have been born again not of seed which is perishable but imperishable, that is, through the living and abiding word of God. . . . Like newborn babes, long for the pure milk of the word, that by it you may grow in respect to salvation." That is a simple yet profound analogy. We should long for the Word in the same way a baby longs for milk. That's a singular focus—a consuming desire. Babies live for milk. It's their sole source of nourishment. And that is Peter's point: we should be as singularly focused on our need for the Word as a baby is focused on his need for milk. That's how we grow spiritually.

Because God's Word is your source of spiritual strength, the time you spend reading and studying it each day makes you a stronger person. You may not always perceive it, but it is feeding your mind and nourishing your spirit. That's why daily Bible study is so important.

6. Psalm 19:7-9

David used six titles for God's Word: the law of the Lord, the testimony of the Lord, the precepts of the Lord, the commandment of the Lord, the fear of the Lord, and the judgments of the Lord. He described its character as perfect, sure, right, pure, clean, and true.

He also delineated its effects: it restores your soul, makes you wise, rejoices your heart, enlightens your eyes, endures forever (is relevant in every age), and produces righteousness.

The Word trains us in righteousness by imparting right thinking, attitudes, actions, and words. What must we do to benefit from that training process? James said, "Putting aside all filthiness and all that remains of wickedness, in humility *receive the word* implanted" (James 1:21, emphasis added). We must receive instruction from the Word with a pure and submissive heart.

Conclusion

The power and effect of God's Word is tremendous: it is able to impart salvation, provide all you need to live a godly life and fully serve God, cut deeply into your life to reveal your sin, expose false teaching and protect you from it, rebuild your life, and train you in righteousness. That's the power of the Word. It's so successful that the person in whom the Word is at work is "adequate [perfect, complete], equipped for every good work" (2 Tim. 3:17).

We do not need additional revelations, writings, or insights from cultic leaders, gurus, or the world system. All that we need to complete our Christian pilgrimage is revealed in the Bible. If we are to be spiritually noble like the Bereans, we must search the Scriptures daily, for therein lies our spiritual nourishment. It's the tool God uses to refine us to maximum usefulness.

How's Your Spiritual Diet?

We live in a day of overindulgence. That's especially true in the spiritual dimension. Many Christians have fed upon worldly things for so long that they have lost their appetite for the Word of God. Others have accumulated so much biblical knowledge without applying it that they have become apathetic in their devotion to God. What can be done about the apathy and indifference in the church? Perhaps the best we can do is be faithful to proclaim the Word, then pray for a better day.

Things haven't always been this way, and I believe that the Lord will somehow restore the appetite of His people for His truth. But in any event we must be faithful proclaimers of God's Word so that those who do hunger for biblical truth can receive the nourishment they need for spiritual growth.

Our attitude towards the Word should be like that of Mary, who listened "to the Lord's word, seated at His feet" (Luke 10:39). Not a day should pass in which you don't spend time feeding your soul from God's Word.

Perhaps you are not a Christian. If that's the case, you need the Word for salvation (2 Tim. 3:15). Read the New Testament until you know what it means to be saved. Perhaps you are not yet grounded in sound doctrine and don't know how to live the Christian life to its fullest. If that's the case, you need the Word for training and maturing (2 Tim. 3:16-17). Perhaps you are a believer harboring sin in your heart. If that's the case, you need to have the piercing sword of the Word reprove your sin and begin its correcting and training work in your life (2 Tim. 3:16).

No matter where you are in your Christian growth, God's Word is sufficient to equip you for every good work. Are you making full use of it?

Focusing on the Facts

1. How do false religious systems attack Scripture (see p. 60)?
2. God will not tolerate anyone's _____ _____ or _____ His Word in any way (see p. 61).
3. Define "reproof" (2 Tim. 3:16; see pp. 61-62).
4. What two aspects of reproof are illustrated in Scripture (see pp. 62-65)?
5. The writer of Hebrews pictures God's Word as a _____ (Heb. 4:12; see p. 62).
6. Define the term "laid bare" as used in Hebrews 4:13 (see p. 63).
7. What is God's opinion of mediums and spiritists (Isa. 8:19-20; see pp. 64-65)?
8. What commendation was given to the Bereans in Acts 17:11 (see p. 65)?
9. Define "correction" (2 Tim. 3:16; see p. 66).
10. Why is the pruning process necessary in a believer's life (John 15:2; see p. 66)?

11. What instrument does the Father use in the pruning process (John 15:3; see p. 66)?

12. What is the responsibility of one Christian toward another Christian who is sinning (Gal. 6:1; see p. 67)?

13. What does it mean to be trained in righteousness (2 Tim. 3:16; see p. 67)?

14. Why does God discipline His children (Heb. 12:10; see p. 68)?

15. What six titles for God's Word are given in Psalm 19:7-9 (see p. 69)?

16. What must we do to benefit from the training process of God's Word (James 1:21; see p. 69)?

Pondering the Principles

1. Paul prayed that the Colossian believers would know God's will so that they would live holy lives. Read Colossians 1:9-12 and note the results of being filled with (lit., "controlled by") the knowledge of God's will. Thank God for the transforming work of His Word in your life, and be sure to take advantage of every opportunity to study Scripture.

2. In our society, there is an unhealthy fascination with predicting and controlling the future. In their denial of divine revelation, many people have turned to astrology, fortunetelling, horoscopes, and mediums of all types. Sadly, some Christians have unwittingly become involved in such activities as well. How does God feel about this issue? Answer the following questions after reading the suggested passages.

   • How seriously does God regard turning to astrology, fortunetelling, horoscopes, and mediums (see Lev. 19:31; 20:6; Deut. 18:9-12; Isa. 47:12-14)?
   • To whom do all mysteries belong (see Deut. 29:29)?
   • Who reveals mysteries (see Dan. 2:27-28)?
   • What is the source of true revelation (see Isa. 8:20)?
   • What is the biblical test of a true prophet (see Deut. 13:1-4; 18:21-22)?
   • In light of the passages just given, what should be your attitude toward such spiritual activities?

Scripture Index

Topical Index

Alexander the Great, destruction of Tyre, 37-38
Ammon. *See* Prophecy
Apathy, spiritual, 70
Apologetics
  importance of, 22
  works on, 19-20, 22
  See also Scripture, verification of
Astrology. *See* Occultic practices
Astronomy. *See* Science

Babylon. *See* Prophecy
Barclay, William, on "laid bare," 63
Bible. *See* Scripture

Canon, the. *See* Scripture
Chastening. *See* Correction, Reproof, Training
Correction
  definition of, 66
  description of, 66-67
  need for, 71
  See also Reproof

Discipline. *See* Correction, Reproof

Egypt. *See* Prophecy
Evangelism, Scripture and. *See* Scripture
Evidences. *See* Apologetics

False teaching, reproving, 60-61, 64-65
Free, Joseph, different methods of calculating silver, 33-34

Geodesy. *See* Science
Geology. *See* Science
Growth, spiritual. *See* Training

Holiness, Scripture and. *See* Scripture
Holy Spirit
  sword of the, 54
  view on Scripture. *See* Scripture
Hydrology. *See* Science

Inerrancy
  definition of, 10
  infallibility and, 10
  See also Scripture
Infallibility
  definition of, 9
  description of, 9-10
  See also Scripture
Inspiration
  definition of, 24
  dictation theory of, 29-30
  evidence for. *See* Scripture, verification of
  extent of, 27-28, 30-34
  figures of speech and, 32-33
  misunderstandings about, 28-34
  origin of, 26
  process of, 26-27
  theory of partial, 30-34
Isostasy. *See* Science

Jastrow, Robert, orbit of the sun, 17-18
Jesus Christ, view on Scripture. *See* Scripture
Joshua, long day of, 32-33

Knowledge, importance of. *See* Scripture, knowing

MacArthur, John
old Bible by the entrance to his home, 56-57
preface to *Why I Trust the Bible* on the Spirit's ministry, 14-15
Maier, Walter, destruction of Ninevah, 19
Maturity, spiritual. *See* Training
McDowell, Josh, *Evidence That Demands a Verdict*, 20
Mediums. *See* Occultic practices
Meteorology. *See* Science
Moab. *See* Prophecy
Morris, Henry M.
The Biblical Basis for Modern Science, 19
number of stars, 17

Nehemiah, revival under, 49-50
New Testament, the inspiration of, 25-26, 31. *See also* Scripture
Nineveh. *See* Prophecy
Noble, how to be, 65

Occultic practices, evil of, 65, 72
Old Testament, the inspiration of, 25, 28, 30-31, 46. *See also* Scripture

Packer, J. I., lack of certainty in the church, 20
Prophecy
evidence of fulfilled, 19, 21
regarding Ammon, 38
regarding Babylon, 38
regarding Egypt, 19, 38
regarding Moab, 38
regarding Nineveh, 19, 38
regarding Samaria, 38

regarding Sidon, 19
regarding Tyre, 19, 35-38
Psychics. *See* Occultic practices

Reproof
definition of, 61-62
description of, 62-65
need for, 71
See also Correction
Restoration, promise of, 67
Revelation
definition of, 24-25
means of, 25-26
Revival. *See* Nehemiah, revival under

Salvation, Scripture and. *See* Scripture
Samaria. *See* Prophecy
Science
astronomy, 17
geodesy, 18-19
geology, 18-19
hydrology, 16
isostasy, 18
meteorology, 17
thermodynamics, 34-35
Scripture
accuracy of. *See* verification of
adding to, 61
apathy regarding, 70
applying, 39-40, 54-56, 58
authority of, 10-11
canon of, 27, 70
claims of about itself, 9-12, 28-29
completion of, 11
correcting with. *See* Correction
defending, 60-61. *See also* verification of
disciplining with. *See* Correction, Reproof
distorting. *See* adding to

effectiveness of. *See* power of
evangelism and. *See*
    proclaiming
holiness and, 52-53, 63-64
Holy Spirit's view on, 14-15
inerrancy of. *See* Inerrancy
infallibility of. *See* Infallibility
inspiration of. *See* Inspiration
interpreting, 54
Jesus' view on, 13-14, 46-48
knowing, 52-53. *See also*
    studying
New Testament. *See* New
    Testament
obeying. *See* applying
Old Testament. *See* Old
    Testament
power of, 12, 15, 20-21, 39,
    44, 57, 60, 70
priority of, 44-45
proclaiming, 50-51, 55-56, 58,
    70
promises of, 45
prophecy and, 19, 35-39
reproving with. *See* Reproof
responding to, 39, 44-45,
    55-57
revelation of. *See* Revelation
salvation and, 46-51, 70-71
science and, 15-19, 34-35
studying, 39-41, 56, 58, 72.
    See also knowing
sufficiency of, 60-61
teaching. *See* Teaching
training with. *See* Training
transforming power of. *See*
    power of

truthfulness of. *See* verifica-
    tion of
verification of, 12-21, 34-39
work of. *See* Correction, Re-
    proof, Salvation,
    Teaching, Training
Sidon. *See* Prophecy
Spencer, Herbert, the matrix of
    existence, 34
Spiritual maturity. *See* Training
Spiritualists. *See* Occultic
    practices
Stars, number of. *See* Science,
    astronomy
Stoner, Peter, probability of ful-
    filled prophecies, 38-39
Sun, orbit of the. *See* Science,
    astronomy

Teaching
    definition of, 51
    importance of, 52-54
    recipients of, 51-52
    response to, 55-57
    See also Training
Thermodynamics. *See* Science
Thompson, Malcolm H., orbit
    of the sun, 17-18
Training
    definition of, 67
    description of, 67-70
    need for, 71
    See also Teaching
Trench, Richard, on reproof, 62
Tyre. *See* Prophecy

Word of God. *See* Scripture